WILLOW BASKETRY

OF THE AMANA COLONIES

History of a Folk Art
Six Willow Basket Patterns

By Joanna E. Schanz

A small lidded laundry hamper by Richard Seifert, Jr. (1895-1980), at left, and a peeled laundry basket by August Rettig (1893-1959) are shown on the grounds of the Museum of Amana History. These baskets are from private collections. The building in background is a combination wash house and woodshed adjacent to the Museum building, which in communal days was a private residence and community kitchen.

Editors: John Zug, Scott Elledge, and David Duer
Graphic Design by Esther Feske
Photography by Joan Liffring-Zug
Historic photographs from private collections

Front Cover: These are willow baskets that can be made following directions included in this book. They are shown on the grounds of the author's home in West Amana, Iowa, one of the seven historic villages of the Community of True Inspiration. The baskets are by Joanna Schanz. From left, in foregound, are split willow laundry basket, apple-picker, oval Easter basket, and round sample basket without handle. On the basket-maker's bench are a round basket with handle, strawberry-picker, and oval community kitchen basket.

Inside front cover: Laura Kleinmeyer is in the traditional swing of the Amana Colonies with her baskets of willow, reed, and other native materials.

A willow basket, maker unknown, has one iron drop handle. Museum of Amana History collection.

Books by Mail: This book may be ordered by mail for $9.95 postpaid from the Schanz Broom and Basket Shop, West Amana, IA 52357

Typesetting by Type House of Iowa
Printed by Julin Printing Company

Penfield
Press
Iowa City, Iowa

CONTENTS

ABOUT THE AUTHOR

Baskets are more than a hobby to Joanna E. Schanz; they're a way of life. The Iowa native apprenticed with one of the last old-time basketmakers. Her baskets have garnered her a regional and a growing national reputation.

Joanna divides her time between basketry and running several family-owned businesses (including furniture and refinishing shops) with her husband Norman. The traditional willow basketry of the Amana Colonies, where Joanna and her family make their home, is the biggest inspiration behind Joanna's work, but she also experiments with new materials and methods of basketmaking. Lecturing and demonstrating basketry techniques at conventions and arts fairs are among Joanna's many crafts activities.

Her exhibitions include: a one-person show at the Amana Arts Gallery in 1980; the Basketworks Exhibit at the John Michael Kohler Center in Sheboygan, Wisconsin in 1981; the Iowa Artists' Exhibit, "Passing Time and Traditions" in 1982-83; and in 1985 the Galleria Show by the Weaving Workshop in Chicago and the Basketlink Exhibit shown in Chicago, California, and Canada.

Classes Joanna has taught include: teaching for the Amana Arts Guild since 1979; natural basketry classes for Indian Creek Nature Center in Cedar Rapids, Iowa in 1982; teaching basketry to area art teachers 1983-84; a class on willow basketry at the Michigan Basketweavers convention in 1985; and in 1986 an apprenticeship funded by a grant from the Iowa Arts Council, classes for the Natural Basketry Seminar sponsored by the Amana Arts Guild, and in Rome, New York.

DEDICATION

Dedicated to Philip Dickel of Middle Amana, the last active basket-maker of the Amana Colonies, for sharing his knowledge of basket-making, giving willow slips for new cultured willow patches, and for teaching us how to make a basket so the knowledge and skill would not be lost. His help, encouragement, and humor made it a delight to learn.

Kathy Kellenberger, center, is holding wild willow branches for a basket. Philip Dickel, last of the historic basketmakers, is standing, with Joanna Schanz seated on his basket bench. In the foreground is *Mrs. Philip Dickel's large laundry basket of peeled and unpeeled willow. Other baskets include an apple picker and a bushel garden basket.*

ACKNOWLEDGMENTS

Many people have helped make this book a reality by gathering information on the history and lives of the basketmakers of the past. Without their help, this book would not exist.

I would like to express my gratitude to:

The Amana Community School Library for the use of its word processor, which made it easier to write and rewrite;

Lanny Haldy, director of the Museum of Amana History, and the museum staff for their help with the history;

Don Shoup, for information about the history found at the Amana Society business office;

The numerous community members who so generously talked about the basketmakers of the past and shared their old historical baskets;

My family and friends, who kept encouraging me to keep writing and listened to me when I was excited about a new find or information;

My father, who took many pictures that helped to organize my book and give me direction;

Kathy and Laura, who share my love of baskets;

My publisher/photographer and her staff for smoothing out the wrinkles, making reprints of the old photos, and photography.

FOREWORD

Though exact dating is impossible, the folk art of basketry is quite ancient. Basket remnants which have survived in the dry protective caves of the American Southwest have been dated by radiocarbon techniques to an age of nine thousand years. In most regions of the world, prehistoric peoples had available such basic raw materials as grasses, roots, canes, and twigs. Ingenious members of tribes must have discovered the art many thousands of years ago. The origins of these skills and traditions are hidden in the mists of antiquity.

The kinds of basketry practiced in each region can be determined by their particular needs, traditions, and aesthetic considerations, and the variety and suitability of accessible materials. Generally, the hot regions of the world have relied on plaiting; the temperate areas on spiral coiling and twining; and the dry zones of North America, southern Eurasia, and the African savannas on sewed coiling.

The seven Amana Colonies of Iowa have been among the significant areas of basketmaking. With the tradition of basketmaking on the edge of extinction in the Amanas, we are grateful to Joanna Schanz for her pioneering work in studying under the tutelage of the last of the makers of willow baskets — Philip Dickel. She has done an admirable job of tracing the history of the art and craft, and gives eminently clear and specific instructions for learning how to carry on the traditions of the masters of the past. She has also supplied us with invaluable historic photographs of earlier generations in the Amanas, caught in actual scenes of the baskets being used in such mundane tasks as collecting laundry and picking apples.

— Harry Oster

Dr. Oster, professor of English (and Folklore) at the University of Iowa, is a past member of the selection panel of the Folk Arts Panel of the National Endowment for the Arts. He was producer of the Iowa Bicentennial Folklife Festival and a contributor to Passing Time and Traditions: Contemporary Iowa Folk Artists, *published by the Iowa State University Press.*

Amana women are outside working with onions in one of the villages in the early 1900s. The ever-useful basket is on the ground. Note the dirt road and the fences which kept livestock out of yards.

THE HISTORIC AMANA COLONIES OF IOWA

When Joanna Schanz, the author of this book, asked Philip Dickel, the last active basketmaker in the Amana Colonies, to tell her about willow basketry, he replied, "I'll do more than tell you; I'll show you." Thus began the present-day revival of basketweaving in the Amanas and the introduction of old-fashioned basket techniques to an eager new wave of basketmakers.

Amana Colony willow baskets are unique, and so is the history of the villages themselves. Perhaps in order to best appreciate the baskets it is good to know a little of the background and beliefs of the immigrants who originally made and used the baskets.

The history of the Amana people began in Germany in 1714 with Lutheran ministers Eberhard Ludwig Gruber and Johann Friedrich Rock, who believed that God could and would reveal Himself to His people through inspired prophets, as in Biblical days. The new faith struggled and almost died out by 1817, when Michael Kraussert became inspired. Soon afterward, Christian Metz and Barbara Heinemann became inspired. Under their leadership, the sect, known as the Community of True Inspiration, began to flourish once again. Some of the Inspirationists were persecuted for their beliefs; this caused groups to gather where landlords were tolerant. The Ronneburg Castle in Hesse, in what is now West Germany, was the home of the largest group.

In 1842 Christian Metz told his followers he had received a message from God that the Inspirationists should move westward overseas to lands where there would be religious freedom. Between 1843 and 1846 over 800 church members came to North America and founded several villages in New York and Canada, near Buffalo. The members developed a communal way of life, with all persons contributing what they could to the community. There were bakers, furniture makers, leather craftsmen, printers, farmers, basketweavers, and many more. Basketweavers brought their own willow slips, not knowing that usable willows were already growing in the new land.

When rapid growth of the city of Buffalo began to threaten the church's simple communal life in the villages of Ebenezer, Christian Metz was once again guided through inspiration to move westward. Land in the fertile Iowa River valley was chosen and purchased.

The first village was built in Iowa in 1855. It was named Amana, from the book of Solomon, meaning "remain faithful". Between 1855 and 1862 six villages were established and named: Amana, East Amana, Middle Amana, High Amana, West Amana, and South Amana. A seventh village, Homestead, was purchased to give access to the Rock Island Railroad. Each village was largely self-sustaining, with its own blacksmith, carpenter, baker, farmers, kitchen workers, and basketmakers.

People ate in community kitchens and attended church daily. Families lived in large brick, stone, or wood-frame buildings divided into apartments. Children over the age of two first attended *kinderschule*, or preschool, before going on to higher grades. Mothers worked together in the kitchens and kitchen gardens. Rarely was anyone alone. Useful utilitarian skills were emphasized. There was little time or need for the decorative arts. Crafts practiced by women included knitting and crocheting.

Each adult member of the community was assigned a job, craft, or occupation by the church elders. Occupations were passed down from father to son. Basketmaking was assigned to men who could no longer go out into the fields and do hard manual labor.

Willow patches were planted and cultivated in each village. All families received the baskets that they were to use. If your basket wore out, you would go to the basketmaker in your village to request a new basket or have your old one repaired. Many of the baskets had initials painted on the side so their owners could identify the baskets brought in from the fields for repair.

Between 1855 and 1932 many things changed in the seven Amana Colonies. The last inspired leader died in 1883. Telephones, automobiles, and other modern inventions invaded the simple life of the villages. Some young people became frustrated with their opportunities in Amana. Other members were not carrying their share of the work load, but still were receiving all the benefits. Some craftsmen — basketmakers included — were selling their wares to visitors and not turning their profits over to the communal treasury. The church elders and the community realized that a change was necessary.

And so the "Great Change" came about. In 1932 the Amana Community voted, village by village, to dissolve the communal way of life and enter the free-enterprise system. The Amana Society was incorporated to take care of the businesses of the community, and the Amana Church Society was created. The simple church services, customs, beliefs, and readings of inspirations were maintained.

Members began working for wages and were free to decide what occupation they would pursue. Many shops were closed by the Amana Society. Some were never to open again; others lay dormant many years before being revived. Cooper shops (where tubs and barrels were made), wagon shops, and shoemakers' shops all closed, as well as hotels, meat markets, bakeries, kitchens, and smithies. Many other craftsmen, including watchmakers, harness makers, and soap makers also closed shop. A total of 59 businesses had shut their doors by May 2, 1932. Basketshops in each village closed, although a few weavers continued to make baskets to sell. They also repaired willow baskets still in use.

It would be many years before a new basketshop would open. Thirty-nine years after the Great Change, in 1971, Joanna and Norman Schanz built the Broom and Basket Shop in West Amana and the craft of broom-making was revived. The owners put into operation an old broom-making machine last used in 1967 by the last of the traditional broom-makers. Wanting to know more about basketmaking, Joanna approached Philip Dickel, whose knowledge about basketry proved to be invaluable. Philip and Joanna planted a cultured willow patch alongside the shop. Later he showed her how to make a willow basket, from the harvesting of willow branches to the last weave. Joanna soon taught others, and today willow basketweaving is once again alive and well in the Amanas.

An Amana woman holds a laundry basket made of peeled and unpeeled willow in this photograph taken by Fred Kent in the 1930s. She is standing in a grape arbor, a typical architectural detail on the grounds of many Amana residences.

AMANA COLONY WILLOW BASKETS

Basketry is an important part of the heritage of the Amana Colonies. The rediscovery of willow basketmaking means the preservation of part of the past for the future. Today, with so much automation and fast pacing, with nearly everything plastic and artificial, we need the simplicity and naturalness of willow basketry to keep us in touch with yesterday.

Basketmakers were among the many immigrants fleeing Europe to America for religious freedom. Knowledge and skills of basketmaking came chiefly from Germany. In the Amana Colonies, as in Europe, baskets were an important part of daily life.

Three basket styles came with the Amana settlers. The coiled straw basket was used to hold rising bread dough; oval coiled straw baskets with wooden bases were used as sewing and Easter baskets. The split oak basket, made only in South Amana, was used for a variety of purposes.

It is the willow basket, however, that has survived the test of time. Of the three types of baskets, willow ones are the strongest and can be repaired most easily. A unique feature of the Amana willow basket is its removable bottom rim. This rim, attached before the handles, protects the bottom of the basket from the wear and tear of everyday use. If the bottom rim wears off, the basket can be repaired and reused. Handles can also be replaced when broken.

The nineteenth-century Ohio Zoar Community, another communal society, made baskets similar to those of the Amanas. Interestingly, a basket school still exists in Lichtenfels, Germany, where the removable bottom rim or *beigesteckten FuZ* is still taught and used chiefly on big strong baskets.

Willow baskets were used everywhere in the Amanas. Huge baskets held wool and wool products in the woolen mills. Willow baskets in all sizes and shapes went to work in the fields and vegetable gardens. Baskets carried food from the community kitchens to the house-bound. Babies slept in baskets. Smaller versions of the adult baskets were made for children. There were so many baskets and they were so functional, everyone took them for granted. Whenever anyone needed a new basket or a basket repaired, the village basketmaker was available to do the making or mending.

Amana willow baskets are used today throughout the villages. The basketmaking revival has made it possible to repair many of the old baskets which continue to be used, as well as to create new baskets. Willow baskets go to potlucks, serve as Easter baskets and waste-baskets, hold sewing projects, carry wood for fireplaces, and hold laundry. Since the revival of basketmaking, many housewives who still hang their clothes outside to dry have replaced their plastic clothes baskets with sturdy willow baskets. Willow baskets are used in vegetable and flower gardens, too.

No two willow baskets are alike. No forms are used. Shaping is done by the basketmaker, and the weaves are easy to learn. Colors of unpeeled willows are earthy and change with time. The texture and shape of the willow rod invite creativity. Not only are the baskets functional, they are well-shaped and decorative. Using a combination of peeled and unpeeled willow, the basketmaker can create a variety of designs through color.

People need to discover the good feeling of basketweaving. When this author became interested in willow basketry in 1972, Philip Dickel of Middle Amana was the only active basketmaker available to teach. Now the tradition has been carried on to a new generation. It is important for basketmakers to continue sharing their knowledge so the art and craft of willow basketry will not be threatened with extinction once again.

Knitting baskets are waiting on church benches for the knitting class. Early 1900s.

Joanna Schanz gets a lesson from the late Philip Dickel in turning down the removable bottom rim of a willow basket. (1978 photograph by Alan Sieve, The NEWSpapers of Iowa County.)

Initials on the sides of baskets aided families in bringing their own baskets back from the fields. Note the initial on the basket fourth from left. The basket at left was purchased at a village store and was not made in the Amanas. All the rest were made by village basketmakers. Early 1900s.

Baskets aided kitchen garden workers in the Colonies. Note the unpainted buildings. The elders thought it less expensive to replace wood than to buy paint.

Village women are harvesting pole beans from a community kitchen garden in this photograph taken in the early 1900s. The garden basket is in need of top rim repair.

THE MUSEUM OF AMANA HISTORY BASKET COLLECTION

The museum's collection of baskets is extensive. The basket display contains a started basket made and donated by Philip Dickel. Huge harvest baskets used in the communal fields and gardens, laundry baskets, lunch baskets from the community kitchens, and an infant's bassinet illustrate the diversity of uses for which the basketmakers of communal Amana practiced their craft. One round basket illustrates an unusual combination of peeled and unpeeled willows. A rye straw basket and a Schaup basket are included in the display.

Throughout the museum are baskets in the other exhibits, showing the importance of baskets in everyday life. The community sewing room display and the *Strickschule,* or knitting school, show peeled baskets. In the church room exhibit is the *Leibesmahl,* or communion basket, an oval peeled basket. The woodshed houses several garden baskets. The washhouse has wash baskets of peeled and unpeeled willow.

The Museum of Amana History and its library help preserve Amana's past for the community and tell the Amana story to visitors. The museum actively identifies, collects, preserves, and displays artifacts and documents that reveal the history of Amana. Maintained and operated by the Amana Heritage Society, a nonprofit corporation, the museum has been recognized for outstanding efforts by the American Association for State and Local History and by the Iowa State Historical Society.

Three historic nineteenth-century buildings house the collections and exhibits. The library contains manuscripts, published books, and photographs. Because of Amana's religious and communal origins, much of the collection is unique.

These knitting baskets in the photograph above came with the Amana people from Germany to Ebenezer, New York, and then in 1854 to Amana, Iowa.

Baskets originally made in Germany and brought to America in the 1840s are in this historic photograph of a children's knitting class. The basket at the left was made in Amana of peeled and unpeeled willow. Bertha Shambaugh photograph for the Iowa State Historical Society.

In the early 1900s young boys were let out of school to pick apples. The apple-picking baskets used here are a different shape from the apple-picker shape given in the pattern on page 77.

Here are smaller garden baskets of peeled willow, early 1900s. While the women worked in kitchen gardens and community kitchens, men in the Colonies worked at crafts or in the fields.

THE HISTORIC BASKET PHOTOGRAPHS

There are about two dozen historic photographs showing baskets in use in the daily lives of the Amana people before the Great Change in 1932. There are no pre-1900 photographs showing Amana people, let alone basketry. The elders of the religious community did not at that time approve of photography or the decorative arts. There was one exception — the Prestele lithographs by Joseph Prestele and his sons, who primarily depicted vegetable and fruit specimens for catalogs. These all-but-forgotten American lithographers were featured in *Drawn from Nature: The Botanical Art of Joseph Prestele and His Sons*, a book by Charles Van Ravenswaay, published by the Smithsonian Institution Press.

As the bans against photographic images and art were gradually relaxed and influences of the outer world became stronger, several Amana men quietly started taking photographs of their neighbors and villages. Some of their photographs showing people and baskets are reproduced in this book.

Other photographers from nearby cities came to take photographs suitable for black-and-white postcards to sell to Colony visitors and others curious about the Amanas. The children's knitting class with the signs, for example, was obviously staged for a postcard.

The only woman taking photographs of the Amana Colonies and their residents in the early 1900s was Bertha Shambaugh of the Iowa State Historical Society. Bertha rode the Iowa City-to-Homestead train and gave illustrated lantern slide lectures about the Community of True Inspiration and the Amana way of life. A few of her photographs, chiefly those showing children knitting, included baskets.

The Amana people did not consider baskets an art form or collectible, but rather a strictly utilitarian necessity. The photographs in this book from the 1900-32 era show that baskets were used extensively as an aid to gardening, field planting, and harvesting, as well as for picnics.

— Joan Liffring-Zug, Publisher, Penfield Press

Baskets were useful for kitchen workers putting up kraut in each village. Early 1900s.

This photograph was taken before the Great Change in 1932. The oval picnic basket of peeled and unpeeled willow has a handle. Beer and wine were made in the Colonies; in 1985-86 a new beer brewery was founded there.

AMANA

BASKETMAKERS

OF THE PAST

"Baskets were made to be used." — Philip Dickel

Who made the baskets that became a part of Amana Colony tradition? Who harvested and planted and wove the willow into sturdy, functional baskets, many still in use today? Who developed the techniques which are continuing to inspire today's generation of basketweavers?

For the most part, they were old men from the "old country" (Germany or Switzerland). Though no longer able to do hard physical labor, they still had much to offer their villages. Many of them were among the original immigrants who came to Ebenezer, New York from Europe. They eventually came to Iowa with other members of the Community of True Inspiration. Although most have little recorded about their lives, a few are given lively, detailed accounts in the church records. But in the same way that no two baskets are exactly alike, neither are the basketmakers who built the Amana's reputation for fine basketry.

Twinkles come to the eyes of some who reminisce about basketmakers they knew or were related to. Some of the names may be forgotten, but the basketmakers' idiosyncrasies are well-remembered. Further information on basketmakers of the past has come from searching through translated church records, which unfortunately do not always list occupations. Philip Dickel, the last active basketmaker from the pre-1932 era when the Amanas were communal, contributed much to this field of research before his death in 1981.

One well-remembered basketmaker used to leave work early to personally deliver his goods to members' homes, in exchange for a little nip or two of the famous Amana wines. If you were in good standing with this basketmaker, you might receive a peeled white willow basket.

Another basketmaker was known for frequently counting his stock of willows but somehow always missing branches that boys would sneak away to play with. He was also a target of their "knock on the door" trick: A rock tied above the front door was controlled by mischievous boys behind nearby bushes; they would pull the string and cause the rock to summon the basketmaker. He would open the door to find no one there, though he no doubt heard giggling behind the bushes.

Whenever a community member needed a new basket, it was ordered from the village basketmaker. One time a mother sent her son to the local basketmaker to order a new wash basket. After waiting a reasonable length of time, the mother sent her son back to see if the basket was ready. The craftsman replied that if she wanted her basket so quickly she should send him a gallon of wine. When the Amanas were communal, families were allotted twenty gallons of wine a year for each man and twelve gallons a year for each woman. The mother sent the requested gallon. Two weeks later, when she sent her son again, the basketmaker requested another gallon. After this gallon was delivered the mother received her wash basket, and both parties were happy.

Each of the seven colonies had its own willow patches and basketmakers. In East Amana the patch was located beside the cemetery. One woman from that village remembers helping a basketmaker while he waited for a doctor to arrive; he had cut himself badly while harvesting branches from the patch.

The village of Amana had one willow patch by the creek on the north side of town and another close to the railroad depot on the south end. Middle Amana also had two willow patches, one on the north end of town by the orchard (close to where the school is now), and the other to the west, near the old hog barn. The basketshop was in a building that later became a chicken house. It had a wood-burning stove and a trough of water in which willow branches were boiled for peeling. Willows were sometimes taken to the Middle Amana Woolen Mill (the present-day site of Amana Refrigeration Inc.) for boiling in the mill's dye tanks.

Homestead had two willow patches, both at the west end of the village. In many of the baskets made in Homestead, French randing was used at the beginning of the sideweaving, which the weavers placed into the base with the uprights. When the four-rod wale was started, the basketmakers used butt-tip-butt-tip insertion.

The High Amana willow patch was near a creek west of the farm houses at the west end of town. The basketshop was in a wooden building (since demolished) in back of a large sandstone house. The building was divided into two parts, with a carpet-weaving and broom-making shop in one half and the basketshop in the other.

Where the willow patch was in West Amana is not remembered. The basketshop was in a small shop (since demolished) at the north end of the village, between a food-drying shed and the wine-pressing house.

Willow patches were cut once a year "at the ground", which does not really mean at ground-level, but down low. (When translating from German to English, "at the ground" was the best way a few old gentlemen of the Amanas could explain this procedure.) The patches were cut so there would be eyes left for next year's growth.

One characteristic Amana basket is the splint woven basket, which was made in South Amana from 1856 to 1915 by Martin Schaup (1800-1873) and his descendents, Samuel Martin Schaup I (1825-1911), and Tobias Schaup (1836-1915). The Schaups were born in

A Schaup split-oak basket went along on this men's day picnic in the early 1900s.

Ontario, Canada and joined the Community of True Inspiration at Ebenezer, New York in 1845. In 1856 they arrived in Amana, bringing with them their Pennsylvania Dutch background and splint basketweaving. Unfortunately, the craft died with Tobias Schaup. Examples of Schaup baskets can be seen at the Museum of Amana History.

The Schaups became part of a long tradition of Amana basketweavers. Another basketweaver was Marten Trautmann (1816-1884), who came from Switzerland and joined the community in 1834. He became blind in 1854; thirty years later, he died suddenly on his way to evening prayer. (In the Amanas, people met for prayers eleven times a week.)

Saxony, Germany was the birthplace of several Amana basketweavers. Carl F. Miller (1836-1914) came with his family to Middle Amana in 1869, where he worked for the farm department. In his later years he learned to make baskets.

Born in Baden, Germany, Philipp Kippenhan (1839-1913) came to Middle Amana with his mother and siblings in 1867. Later he moved to South Amana and wove willow baskets there, also working on the South Farm.

Villagers still remember the white hair and beard of John Hug (1847-1939). He was the High Amana basketmaker and lived in the High Amana church building. John was born in Switzerland.

An oval willow basket made by John Hug is in a private collection.   *The initials P.K. are for the Pitz Community Kitchen.*

The baby basket at left, made by Ludvig Dittrich, is in his descendants' collection. The basket at right came from Germany.

Field workers are shown having lunch in the early 1900s. Ludvig Dittrich was noted for oval baskets like these.

Ludvig Dittrich (1852-1937) was noted for his pipe and homemade tobacco, as well as for teaching Richard Seifert of Homestead to make baskets. Born in Hussen, Germany, Ludvig came to Amana in 1884 with his father. He was a mason as well as basketmaker.

Gustav Schaedlich (1859-1935) was a basketmaker in West Amana. He was born in Saxony, as was Louis Carl Krauss (1860-1938). Louis came to Amana with his parents in 1867, left the community in 1888 to marry Marie A. Christen, returned in 1889, and remained until his death.

Saxony was also the birthplace of Ernest Heidel (1864-1924) and Max Moessner (1867-1925), both of whom made baskets in Middle Amana. Other basketmakers included Emil Kellenberger (1866-1922) of West Amana and Fritz Christen (1867-1947) of Amana. One of Emil's daughters remembers that he made baskets for a short time in High Amana before his death. A growth on his neck had confined him to a wheel chair.

The neat and well-shaped baskets of Alvin Werner (1869-1931) prove that he was a perfectionist. Slewing was sometimes used in place of French randing. Wooden handles were wrapped with fancy weaves. Removable bottom rim spokes were used on the outside for added design. Alvin liked to color some peeled willows with dye from the woolen mill; purple was his favorite color. Only a few rows were colored, as he was also conservative.

A round Easter basket by Alvin Werner shows decorative use of the bottom rim uprights. The background shows the traditional grape trellis at the Museum of Amana History. (Schanz collection.)

Rye straw was used to make the coiled baskets used by the village bakeries for dough-rising. Early 1900s.

A native of Saxony, Alvin moved to East Amana and married Milda Mehlem there in 1897; they had one daughter. Alvin loved to work in the kitchen garden and was in charge of the potato field and the willow patch. Most of his basketry was done in the winter months. He harvested, sorted, and stored willows for use when needed.

By 1929 Alvin was in poor health and the elders of the community assigned Otto Bahndorf to study basketry under him. The elder craftsman died of cancer.

Louis Schmieder of Amana remembers as a small boy accompanying his father, the Amana baker, to the rye fields before harvesting. They selected the longest and nicest rye straw they could find. Once cleaned, the straw was taken to Robert Salzbrenner (1874-1934) to make into dough-rising baskets for the Amana bakery.

Although Carl Kiesling (1881-1938) is listed in church records as a custodian, he was also the basketmaker who taught Philip Dickel. Carl was the last of the basketmakers born in Saxony; he came to the Colonies with his parents sometime in the 1880s.

It took a lot of strength to spread the base spokes of a basket and Carl was not particularly fond of this aspect of weaving. Quite often he would use the softer wild willow for base spokes.

An oval willow basket made by Carl Kiesling is in his descendants' collection. The wooden shovel in background is in the collection of the Museum of Amana History.

Louise Zuber hides behind slough grass collected for basketmaking in 1920 by her father, William F. Zuber.

In the fall, William F. Zuber (1886-1960) collected slough grass, tied it into bundles, and stored the bundles in a woodshed until he was ready to use them. After soaking the slough grass, the beginning of the coiled basket was tied in place with string off flour sacks. This held the center of the coil in place while the binder of cane could be started. Very few of these coiled straw baskets are found today, although William made many coiled dough-rising baskets and repaired many other old ones.

August W. Rettig (1893-1959) was a butcher in Middle Amana until he became ill with pneumonia in the late 1920s. After recovering, August was assigned to work in the basketshop with Carl Kiesling. Work in the shop was dry and warm and would not tire out someone who had had a bout with pneumonia. (Note: His laundry basket is shown on the title page.)

When the Middle Amana basketshop and other shops were closed in 1932 because of the Great Change from religious communal life to free enterprise, August worked for the farm department, in charge of laborers. He also ran the milk route for a short time. During the winter months, however, he continued to make baskets.

In 1941, just before the war, August started working for the Amana Refrigeration factory in Middle Amana. After retiring, August again picked wild willows and started weaving baskets.

He sold baskets to Killian's Department Store in Cedar Rapids, Iowa, just twenty miles from the Amana Colonies. However, the store manager wanted all the baskets to be exactly alike in size and shape. August found this frustrating because it is impossible for handmade baskets to be exactly alike. Shape is controlled by the weaver and forms are not used. Size is determined by the size of willows harvested.

August, who married Susanna Graft in 1917, sold baskets to the Homestead Sandwich Shop and offered baskets for sale at his house. August kept returning to basketmaking throughout his life because he enjoyed working with willow. His two children, Leonard and Betty Rettig Parvin, live in Middle Amana.

This author had the opportunity to repair one of August's "sold at home" baskets shortly after learning how to make baskets. A woman from Oxford, Iowa brought in a round basket to have the handle repaired. The basket was her favorite and most-used. It was, as she put it, "just perfect to hold my round casserole dish and plate to take to church potlucks."

A lifelong bachelor, Richard Seifert Jr. (1895-1980) learned how to make baskets from Ludvig Dittrich in Amana and Alvin Werner in East Amana. After the Great Change in 1932, when the basketshops were closed, Richard continued to make a few baskets in Homestead and was always willing to do the mending of old baskets for the village residents. He worked for the woolen mill and the farm department. In his later years, when he was not making baskets, he always surrounded himself with them in his hallways and rooms, hanging others on the walls, where they were handy when he wanted to use them. (Note: His small lidded laundry hamper is shown on the title page.)

The son of basketmaker Louis Carl Krauss, David Krauss (1904-1965) made a few baskets himself and started a cultured willow patch along the railroad on the west side of Homestead. He married Helen Seifert in 1924, and they had four children.

A large lidded willow laundry hamper made by Otto Bahndorf is in a private collection. The Museum of Amana History is in the background.

Otto Bahndorf, who was born in East Amana in 1904, learned his craft in 1929 and worked at it until 1932, when the basketshop in East Amana was closed. At 28, Otto worked first for the Amana Society farm department, later for the woolen mill, and then as a carpenter.

During his apprenticeship to Alvin Werner, Otto remembers, his teacher was sick for a time. One woman came to the basketshop to have a handle repaired. Alvin said he would do the repair when he felt better. When the woman returned some time later, insisting she had to have the handle repaired soon, Otto decided to try. In the process of learning how to twist the willow to make it pliable enough to wrap around the handle spoke, he broke a couple of the willow branches. Alvin reprimanded Otto severely for attempting the repair. Although Otto had done a good repair job, Alvin told him he should not have wasted so many willows. Alvin always kept an attic full of willows, but he was typically thrifty and did not want to waste even a couple.

Otto's favorite basket was the shaped clothes basket with a lid. He called it the "milk can basket" because of its unusual shape. Despite having made baskets only a few years, the lifelong bachelor still talks about his basketmaking experiences with fondness. If the basketshop had not closed, he might have continued to make baskets for many more years. "Well," he said recently, "we had to make a living and do what was needed." While many people missed the security of the communal way of life, they realized the times demanded economic change.

Another basketmaker is Carl Metz of Middle Amana, who was born in 1917. Carl used to be in charge of a farm department potato field. When he needed field baskets, basketmakers Carl Kiesling and August Rettig told him that if he would make the bases, they would finish the baskets. And so Carl learned how to make baskets, using his knee to shape the bases. To help shape their bases so they curved upward, his teachers used discs from farm machinery instead of their knees. Carl also made a few baskets for his own use.

"Baskets were made to be used," Philip Dickel (1899-1981) used to tell the people he gave his baskets to. When he gave Joanna Schanz, the author of this book, one of his bushel-sized baskets he made her promise to use it and not put it in a corner to look at. Philip never sold any of his baskets, but gave them all away.

Prior to 1932, Philip had worked in Middle Amana, where he was born, at his assigned job of bookbinding. He married Elizabeth C. Schaedlich in 1925, and they had three children. To learn basket-making, he would visit Carl Kiesling in the evenings.

After the Great Change of 1932, Philip planted his own willow patch and continued to weave in his spare time. During this period he worked in the carding department of the Amana Woolen Mill and was a night watchman at the Amana Refrigeration plant. Retire-

Today this small oval basket, made in the Amanas prior to the Great Change from religious communal life, is used primarily to hold clothespins. The scene is South Amana in 1968. Joan Liffring-Zug photograph.

ment years found him working as custodian for the Amana schools.

Philip Dickel brought traditional Amana basketry to the current generation of basketmakers. In 1973 he gave willow slips to Joanna Schanz to plant. Four years later he taught her how to harvest and sort willows and how to make traditional Amana Colony willow baskets. Philip was delighted to have someone reviving his craft of basketmaking. Even if he didn't know the names of the weaves and techniques he taught (that information could be found in books on basketry), he was an expert.

Each year after 1977, Philip would join Joanna Schanz and Kathy Kellenberger at arts festivals and demonstrations throughout Iowa, talking, exhibiting their wares, and delighting the crowd. Several newspaper articles were printed about Philip and the revival of basketmaking. Once, to impress upon a newspaper reporter how strong the baskets he made were, Philip stood on the removable bottom rim of a basket he had just completed.

Shortly before he died in 1981, the Amana Arts Guild presented Philip Dickel with its "Friend of the Arts" award for sharing his knowledge and promoting the art of basketry. His presence is felt — and his admonition to use baskets, not just display them — is remembered every time this author and her friends sit down to weave.

BASKETMAKERS
OF TODAY

Traditionally, men were the Amana basketweavers, but today the typical Amana basketmaker is a woman. Baskets are still used in the old ways, whether for toting laundry, picking apples, or other purposes. A few of today's basketweavers are introduced here, along with some of their children — possibly the young basketmakers of tomorrow.

WEST AMANA

Norman Schanz had a challenge for his wife: to make a giant basket to go with the eleven-foot solid walnut rocker in their West Amana Schanz Furniture and Refinishing Shop. The huge rocker is well-known regionally, and was once displayed at the Iowa State Fair. Daunting as the challenge was, Joanna Schanz, the author of this book, accepted it.

Joanna was prepared because she had been working with willow basketry since she planted her first cultured willow patch outside the Broom and Basket Shop in West Amana in 1972. In 1977, Philip Dickel, the last active basketweaver in the Colonies, gave her personal basket-weaving lessons. The master and his apprentice exhibited their work together and gave weaving demonstrations at local arts festivals for several years. By 1979 Joanna was teaching her own classes.

"Having a very understanding family has certainly been a big help," Joanna says of her work with willows, which can indeed be demanding on a household. Her four children — Jolene, Kathy, Mike, and Marsha — have put up with willows and wild branches soaking in the bathtub. They have hiked across muddy fields to find willow patches, and they always find the basement messy with materials.

Joanna makes different types of baskets for every season: "Spring fever" baskets are woven out of cuttings from bushes and trees found in her own back yard, including lilac, dogwood, honeysuckle, mock orange, mulberry, and, of course, willow. Summer finds

Joanna weaving with crab apple branches and willow. In the fall, she makes baskets out of bittersweet and willow. Winter baskets are made out of dogwood, grapevine, and willow. Although making traditional cultured and wild willow baskets is still Joanna's main concern, she likes to experiment with all the natural materials that her back yard and the surrounding countryside have to offer. She also likes trying new weaving techniques and demonstrating those that work well to her students.

Besides teaching, Joanna lectures and demonstrates weaving throughout the United States. One of her baskets was chosen for the 1982-83 Iowa Folk Art traveling exhibit, "Passing Time and Traditions". Another basket was in the Basketry Link Exhibition in 1985 in Chicago, Illinois; Mendocino, California; and Vancouver, British Columbia.

Born in Cedar Rapids, Iowa in 1942, Joanna Conrad was married in 1961 to Norman Schanz of West Amana. Their businesses are located in Amana, West Amana, and South Amana.

The enormous basket which Norman challenged Joanna to make was begun in August 1984 during the Amana Arts Guild Arts Festival and finished in October of that same year. The basket is 36 inches round and 39 inches high. And, as Norman promised his wife, the basket now has a home next to the famous giant rocker.

SOUTH AMANA

It took only one willow basket for Kathy Augustine Kellenberger to fall in love with weaving. She started in Joanna Schanz's basketry class in 1979 and discovered she had an aptitude for weaving. One year and many baskets later she returned to class as a teacher and has been teaching with Joanna since.

Kathy is a typically busy — some would say obsessed — weaver. One day she was babysitting with two in diapers, cooking chili, baking a cake, and boiling willows for peeling in a large canner — all at the same time! Her oldest daughter came home from school, opened the door to a variety of smells, and said, "I hope that's not supper!"

Working with willows has nevertheless inspired Kathy's daughter Beth. At age nine, Beth started picking up the tip ends which her mother was discarding on the floor. Beth wove a little basket on her own and won a blue ribbon at the 4-H fair.

Kathy Kellenberger is holding her basket of peeled and unpeeled willow which appeared in the Basketry Link exhibition.

A collection of Kathy Kellenberger's baskets are in front of her workshop.

Laura Kleinmeyer holds her eggbasket of reeds and grapevines. Background is the main street of Amana. The lamp is a Bill Metz replica of the original lanterns of the Amana Colonies.

Beth and her sister Emily, as well as Kathy's husband Patrick (they were married in 1972), accompany Kathy on willow-cutting expeditions and keep an eye out for new wild willow patches. Pat helped his wife plant and cultivate her first cultured willows in their back yard in 1980. Without her family's support, says Kathy, working with willow basketry would not be so much fun. They live in the old Kellenberger family home in Upper South Amana.

Using mostly cultured or wild willow, Kathy makes traditional Amana Colony shapes and sizes. She specializes in (and has the patience for) willow miniatures. Kathy, who was born in Estherville, Iowa in 1951, experiments with peeling willow. In both 1982 and 1983 she had a basket chosen for the Iowa Folk Arts traveling exhibition, "Passing Time and Traditions". The Basketry Link Exhibition in 1985 displayed another of her baskets.

HOMESTEAD

When Laura Sandersfeld Kleinmeyer's son Nathan was a preschooler, he wanted to help his mother with her basketweaving. "Will this work?" he would ask — and still does — as he searches about for materials that could be used in weaving baskets. He, his father Dennis, and his brother Joshua help Laura on wild willow and grapevine cutting expeditions. Nathan now owns his own pair of willow clippers.

Laura, an Iowa farm girl born in 1958, is another basketmaker who learned her craft from Joanna Schanz. She was a salesclerk in the Schanz furniture store in West Amana when she began taking lessons in 1978. Today she continues in sales and management at the store and weaves at home in Homestead (one of the seven villages of the Amana Colonies) on her days off.

Besides willow, Laura works with grapevine, dogwood, and other natural materials — and experiments with reeds, rushes, denim, and rawhide. She tries out natural dyes on some of her reed and rib-style baskets. Joshua likes to help dyeing reeds and has a good eye for finding berries from which to make dyes. The boys willingly share their wading pool with their mother's willows and reeds.

INNOVATIONS BY TODAY'S WEAVERS

Many of the old, basic weaving techniques have been improved upon by Joanna, Kathy, and Laura. Combining Amana Colony basket techniques with other techniques has enabled the basket-makers of today to create nontraditional baskets and one-of-a-kind willow baskets. Use of natural materials other than willow also makes for interesting baskets.

Traditionally, wall baskets were not made. Today, rib-style willow wall baskets are often created. Using the Amana techniques, wall baskets with removable bottom rims are fashioned so that they have a flat side against the wall. It is also possible to make willow fishing creels for sportsmen.

A thick grapevine twisted into a hoop becomes the handle in an Amana willow basket. The handle is woven into the base and with the sides. The odd-shaped handle determines the shape of the finished basket for a unique container. The bottom rim is removable.

The beginning of the weaving of an oval base and the directions given in this book are examples of the improvements of the basket-makers of today. When the base spokes are bound together with the split willow, the split willow continues to weave in between the spokes and is not "Xed" out. Alternating butt and tip ends in side-weaving four-rod wale and three-rod wale was traditionally used only in Homestead baskets. Such alternation is used today to allow the shorter wild willow to be used to make a basket with even sides.

Using a combination of peeled and unpeeled willow allows for more flexibility and creativity. Variations of French randing also expand the weaver's options. A sculptured basket can be created by weaving another basket onto a completed basket where the removable bottom rim should be.

Joanna, Kathy, and Laura weave their more traditional baskets using historic Amana Colony baskets as their guides. Their new baskets are sold through the Schanz Broom and Basket Shop in Main Amana and each year at the Amana Arts Festival held in Middle Amana the second Saturday in August. Each basketmaker also takes special orders.

In the spring, many of the old baskets are repaired to extend their usefulness. Bottom rims are replaced, new handles are put on, and top rims are mended. About the only thing that cannot be repaired is the bottom of the basket, which is why the removable bottom rim is important. It makes it possible to reuse a basket when only the bottom rim has worn out.

BASKETMAKING MATERIALS

Newly planted cultured willow patches are maintained by the basketmakers. Once a year, after the leaves have fallen, but before buds appear, the willow is harvested, sorted, and stored for later use.

One never knows where a good willow patch or other weavable material may be found, so pruning shears are never far from the hands of the basketmakers: in back pockets, in purses (have you ever had to explain to airport security what those shears are for?), under car seats, and even in diaper bags. Basketmakers have found material in ditches along the road, near shopping malls, along interstates, and next to houses or buildings in large cities.

One of the joys of basketmaking is finding weavable material and creating a souvenir of a good time. An inner tube trip down the Apple River in Wisconsin was the inspiration to create a basket incorporating roots from the trees along the banks, as well as bits of inner tubing and twine used to tie the tubes together. Grapevine, poplar twigs, and a form of dogwood picked near a motel in Galesburg, Illinois became a memento of a happy trip. But sometimes basketmakers gather more than memories and willows out in the fields: One of the women once found herself in a patch of poison oak, instead of willow. Bittersweet times, however, lend themselves to sweet memories.

TOOLS

Pruning shears
Pocket knife
Wide flat-head round screwdriver (not a Phillips)
Strong awl
Round wooden pounding stick

Optional tools
Willow brake — Two smooth metal rods sprung together. Willow rod is drawn through to peel willow.
Knife block — A heavy knife blade mounted on a wooden board. Split willow is drawn through the knife, which is set to different thicknesses, to make the split willow smooth and uniform in size.

Equipment
Work board — thick, 14-inch-square plywood
Clothespin or marker
Shoestring or strong cord
Five-gallon bucket for wild willows
55-gallon drum for cultured willows

Shoestring, round fat screwdriver, pounding stick (any round, heavy piece of wood is suitable), clip *clothespin, fat round awl, pocket knife, pruning shears. Note hole in center of workboard where basket is spiked down for working.*

WILLOWS
AND WILLOW PATCHES

CULTURED WILLOWS

All willows have a butt, tip, back, and belly.

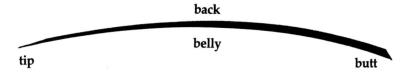

back

belly

tip   **butt**

To the best of our knowledge, the willow originally cultured in the Amana Colonies was the *Salix Nigra* (one of the black varieties). This is the cultured willow used today.

Planting and care — The butt end of a willow is cut about twelve inches long and planted with a couple of eyes pointing upward. Position four willow cuttings in an eighteen-inch square with a fifth willow cutting in the center of the square.

18 inches 18 inches

The willows will be forced to grow up and straight. Cuttings can be planted in the fall, but you may have better luck by rooting the cuttings and planting in the early spring. Because cultured willows do not send out roots, where you plant your cutting is where your cultured willow bush will be.

Ground should be well-cultivated and kept weeded the first three years. Watering during drought periods is necessary until the patch is well established. Mulching is helpful to those of us who have limited garden time or patience. By the third year your patch should be producing enough for basketmaking.

Cutting — Cut your cultured willows after a killing frost when the leaves have fallen off and before the spring buds appear. No sap is running at this time and you will not harm your cultured willow patch. Cut each branch, leaving a couple of eyes for next year's growth. Lay the willow butt ends together in a pile ready to sort.

Sorting — Gather a big armful of willows and place butt ends into a container tall enough to hold the willows. Usually a 55-gallon drum or barrel is needed for the tall cultured willows. Shake the willows down so that all the butt ends are at the bottom of the barrel. Gently gather at the top and pull out only the tallest willows. Place these willows on a pile. Shake down the willows again and pull out the tallest ones. Put these either on the same pile as the first willows or start a new pile if the willows are noticeably shorter. Continue shaking down, gathering, pulling out the tallest, and piling until you have sorted all the willows. Sort by length, not thickness. Tie up your sorted willows and store until ready to use.

Storing — Store away from the sun, heat, and wind, any of which will dry the willows. The north side of a building, providing protection from the sun and wind, is a good place for storing covered willows. Inside an unheated building away from windows is another possibility, as are your freezer or root cellar. If willows become frozen, they can be thawed and used. If your willows should dry out, they can be soaked and used.

Soaking — Soak from one to five days, depending on the thickness and the dryness. Any container that you can fit your willows into is usable. Stock tanks, children's wading pools, bathtubs, or a nearby creek are all good places. Willows float, so they need to be weighted down.

Count and select the willows you want to use and soak only those willows. Repeated soaking and drying of willows may discolor or weaken them.

Selecting — Carefully select the willows you plan to use in a basket. Place the sorted willow piles on the ground. Look through the center of the pile to select willows of the thickness you want to use for each step. To allow for broken willows, select several more than you think you will be using.

WILD WILLOWS

When cultured willows are not available, or for your first "learning" baskets while your cultured patch is growing, wild willows can be used with good results. Wild willow is not as strong as the cultured because it will not have as much wood.

Where to find — Look for the bush willow, not the weeping willow tree. Look along river banks, on sand bars, in moist road ditches, and low-lying farm fields. Wild willow likes moisture and sun. Ask your county weed commissioner, conservation officer, county extension service, local deer hunter, or anyone who may know where wild willow patches are.

Spring and summer willow will be green and will be budding or have leaves. Fall willows will be reddish and may or may not have leaves. Winter willows are the easiest to locate because their reddish color stands out from the snow-white background.

A patch may look like a good patch from the road, but when you walk up to it, may turn out to be an old overgrown patch. The ideal wild willow patch is one with a lot of one-year growth coming up out of the ground. Wild willow sends roots upward, and these roots spread.

When you locate a good usable patch, always get permission from the land owner and cut correctly so that you will be welcome to come back. A nice Thank You to the landowner is one of your baskets.

Cutting — Wild willow can be cut any time of year. It is hard to kill a wild willow patch. Be sure you know the hazards before you go out to cut.

Cut the long slender willows. Stop at one willow bush and cut all the usable willows by following the willow from the tip end to the butt end, leaving eyes for next year. Cut nothing fatter than a pencil. After you have cut all the usable willow from that bush and piled butt ends together, cut down the fat unusable willow and leave them lay. Next year when you come back to the patch, you will have more to pick. Tie your usable willows in bundles that you can handle and take home to sort.

Sorting — Place one of your tied wild willow bundles in a five-gallon bucket and cut the tie off. Shake down the willows so that all the butt ends are at the bottom of the bucket. Gently gather at the top and pull out only the tallest willows. Place in a pile. Shake down again and pull out the tallest ones. Place these either on the same pile with the first group or start a new pile if the willows are noticeably shorter. Continue to shake down, gather, pull out the tall ones, and pile until you have sorted all the willows. Sort by length, not thickness. Tie your sorted piles and store till used.

Storing — The storing rules for cultured and wild willow are the same. Store away from the sun, heat, and wind, which are drying to willows. The north side of a building, providing protection from the sun and wind, is a good place for storing covered willows. Inside an unheated building away from sunlight is also a good storage place. Forgotten green willows stored and left unstirred will tend to mold, change color, and soften. If your willows should dry out, they can be soaked and used.

Soaking — When soaking wild willow, be sure that there are absolutely no leaves or foliage on the stems to spoil your water. Strip all the leaves off before soaking. Soaking time will depend on the dryness and thickness. Soak as you would cultured willows.

Selecting — Before soaking, always select the willows you want to put into your basket. With the wild willow you will be using what you have picked from nature, and that may add character to your basket. You will find it helpful to look through the middle of your sorted piles for the thickness you need. You can spot a variety of thicknesses.

Hazards — Enjoy nature as you work in the wild willow patch. But, along with the quiet, peace, and earthy smells, you should be aware of some of the hazards.

The month of June is a risky time because the red-wing blackbirds are nesting. The birds will warn you and swoop down on you if you approach and venture too close to their nesting area.

Early morning and dusk are animal times. Skunks have been smelled, although this author has not yet seen one. Deer, raccoon, and rabbit leave their droppings behind to be stepped in, knelt on, and sat in. Snakes have been spotted sunning themselves from tops of willow bushes. When the willow patch is partially in water, splashes have been heard, but this author has not stayed around to find out what did the splashing.

When it is the hunting season do not go hunting for willows. If you must go, dress like a hunter so you will not be mistaken for a deer. Expect the unexpected and do not forget that you are in Nature's domain. Go with a friend or be sure someone knows where you are going and when you will be returning.

PEELING WILLOWS

We have found several ways to successfully peel the skin off willows to make white willows. White willows tend to dry out fast after they have been peeled and usually have to be soaked before using.

Boiling — Willows can be softened by coiling into a large canner and boiling. How long to boil depends on the thickness of your willow. After boiling, let willows soak in the water until they cool down. Color may be buff. Peel and store for later use.

Peeling by hand when the sap is running — By checking the willow patch each day in the early spring or fall, you can catch the willow when the sap is running up or down. The skin will peel off very easily. Start at the butt end, make three strips, and pull down to the tip. A willow brake tool will save time, but may damage the willow.

Peeling by hand when there is no sap running — Scrape the skin with a pocket knife, starting from the butt end.

Pitting — In winter, stand bundles of sorted fresh willows in six inches of water. In the spring when the sap starts to rise, the willow can be easily peeled by hand or willow brake.

AN AMANA COLONY ROUND WILLOW BASKET

Step-by-step sample basket

It is recommended that you make a simple round willow basket to learn the techniques and get the feel of working with willow. Willow baskets are not hard to make. The weaving techniques are easy and you may know the techniques by other names. It will take from twelve to fourteen hours from harvesting to completed willow basket. When you are done, you will have a better appreciation for baskets, a handy basket for your use, and a desire to make another basket out of willow. There will not be another basket like yours. It will have charm and character. As one student said after completing her willow basket, "I'm going to take it home and love it."

ROUND BASE

Select and cut six straight base spokes ⅜ inch in diameter and 10 inches long from the butt end of your willows. Three base spokes will need to be split in the middle. Push your pocket knife through the middle of one base spoke and give the knife a twist to open the middle of that spoke. Insert three spokes through the opening. Open two more spokes and put the same three inserted spokes through the splices. If any of your base spokes has a noticeably slim end, watch so that the slim end is next to a fat end when you insert your spokes. You should have three base spokes inserted in the middle of three base spokes.

Base spokes (three spokes inside of three)

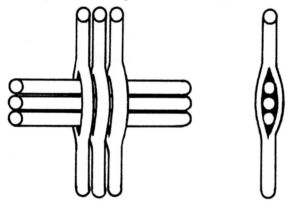

Splitting willows — Select one long, slim, straight willow without any defects to be split in half. Starting with the tip end, split the selected willow with your pocketknife ½ inch and finish splitting by hand. Easiest hand position is to hold the split ends with your thumb and middle finger using your index finger as a pressure point when you move down the willow, pulling the willow apart as you go. When the split goes off to one side, put more pressure on the opposite side to force the split to straighten out. You will be using both pieces of the split willow.

There are two times when you may want to use split willows in your basket. The first is, as above, when you need the split willow to hold your base spokes together before you start weaving. The second is when you have nice willows that are too fat to use as weavers. Fat willows without defects can be split and used in weaving French randing. Take care in selecting willows to be split. Pick willows that have no branch scars and other defects to split around.

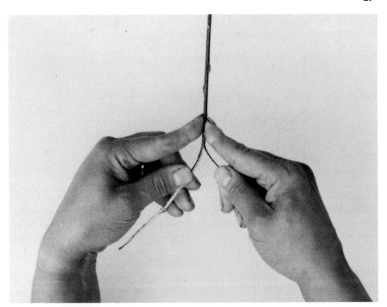

Hand position when splitting a willow

Inserting base split weavers — Insert both tip ends of the split willow together into the same split of the base spokes to help hold the weavers in place when you start to weave. You will be twining over the four sets of base spokes. To get ready to twine, you must move one of the spliced weavers up and over to the right of one set of base spokes. You now have two spliced weavers hanging down from two different sets of base spokes. As you twine you want to keep the skin side out and the raw spliced side in so it does not show. This will be hard the first time.

Twining — Pick up the weaver on the left side, go under the base set of three spokes, coming up between the sets of spokes and on top of the other weaver, go over the top of the next set of three base spokes and back down between the sets of spokes. Pick up the other weaver which is now in the left-hand position and weave across the bottom of the base set of three, up between the sets crossing over and, holding the other weaver in place, over the top of the next base set, and down between the set and let hang. Pick up left weaver and weave as before: under set of three, between sets, over set of three and hang down. You will probably have to hold the hanging weaver in place with your thumb until the other weaver crosses over and holds it in place. Weave three rows to hold the base spokes together.

Turn the base over and tuck the two ends under two different weaver wrappings, forming an "X". Cut split weavers short.

Twining over four sets of base spokes

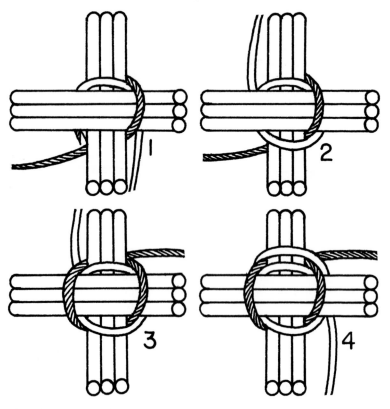

Start two tip ends of two slim full willow weavers and twine between each base spoke, starting to spread the spokes evenly. Do not bend or spread the center base spokes, as they should stay straight. Only the side spokes should be spread and moved. You will want to continue twining with two full weavers, replacing the weavers with the tip end of a new weaver when you feel that the weavers are getting too fat, but try to replace them at different times. It is important to get the base spokes evenly spaced as soon as possible. Twine a few rows until your spokes are evenly spaced and you have enough room to do double twining.

Twining between each base spoke

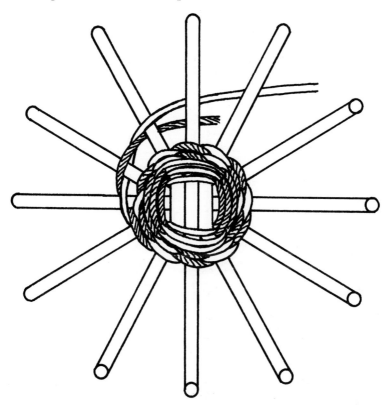

Double twining — When your spokes are evenly spaced and you have enough room and are about in the middle of a weaver, add the tip end of a new weaver to the weaver you are using and use the two as one, continuing the twining. Both weavers should have the tip of a new weaver added so that you are twining with two sets of weavers. Each set of weavers has a skinny weaver and a fat weaver, which you are treating as one weaver when you twine. Keep the skinny weaver toward the center of your basket base on the top side and flat between the spokes. What the skinny weaver is doing is taking up space between the rows covering the base spokes so that you have a fuller, neater base.

When the fat weaver becomes too fat, insert a new tip so the new weaver becomes the skinny weaver, the old skinny weaver becomes the fat weaver, and the old fat weaver is dropped. If the dropped fat weaver is too long and getting in your way, cut some off, but do not

Double Twining

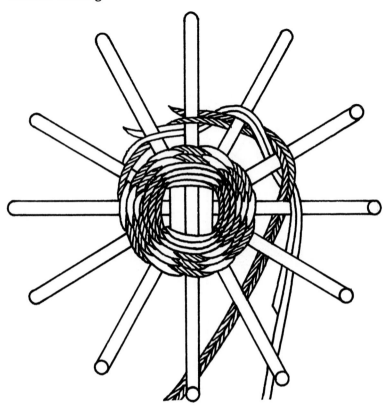

cut or trim close until you have completed the whole base. Try not to add new weavers at the same time. Double twine until you come to the shortest base spoke.

Ending base weavers — To end your weavers you need to weave one of the last weavers a couple spokes more and tuck in between rows. Then weave the other weaver one more spoke and tuck in between the weaving rows.

Trimming the base — You need to trim the tip ends that are on the top of your base, which will be the inside of your basket. You need to trim the butt ends that are sticking out the bottom side of your base. Remember to trim at a slant and be sure the ends have a spoke to rest against so that the weavers will not pop out of place in your weaving. If any of the base spokes are sticking out, you need to trim them close to the weaving. Your base is now completed and ready to put on your spiked bench or board.

Completed base

About bases — Bases can be made and saved to be used later. You can use peeled and unpeeled willows in your base for color variations. Smaller baskets would be started with base spokes arranged two inside of two spokes. Larger baskets would use an arrangement of four spokes inside of four spokes. You can use almost any combination, but these are the main ones used in the Amana Colony-style basket.

When you are first learning to make an Amana Colony-style basket, the base is the hardest and takes the longest time, though it is the first thing you have to make. Remember, once the side uprights are inserted, the real fun begins with the side weaving.

UPRIGHTS

Select 24 straight willows that are about ¼ to ⅜ inches in diameter at the butt end and 34 to 36 inches long. Taper-cut the butt end. Carefully insert one upright on each side of a base spoke, making sure that the upright goes into the base far enough to stay in place while you are weaving. Uprights should not poke out the bottom of your base. Try to get the uprights inserted as close to the center of your base as possible; one and one-half to three inches is far enough for a ten-inch base.

Inserting uprights (top view)

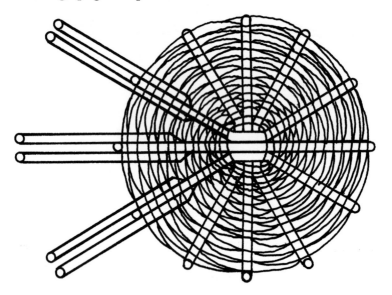

Inserting uprights (side view)

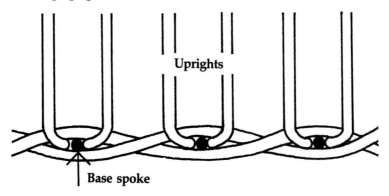

After each willow is inserted, lay a fat round screwdriver on top of the upright outside the base and bend the upright upward. If the willow upright breaks, pull it out, taper-cut it off, and try again. If the willow upright breaks the third time, throw that willow away and select a replacement.

After all 24 willow uprights are inserted, gather the uprights up two by two in a teepee fashion. Lay each new set of two uprights on top of the last set of two. Tie tightly near the top, making sure the tie is directly above the center of your basket. The teepee tie helps you shape the basket sides. By moving the tie down you can shape the sides inward. By moving the tie up you can shape the sides outward. If you want to really flare the sides of your basket, you can untie the top and let the uprights flare out after a few rows of weaving. Uprights are harder to control when untied. You can also twine a heavy cord between the uprights at about the middle of the basket to help control the flare. Willows are harder to handle and shape than reeds. You may find that you have to really pull your tie inward to get the inward shaping you want, or you may have to untie to get the flare outward that you want to achieve. It may take drastic shaping to get what you have in mind. Willows do not stay where you put them! You always have to be working on the shape.

Following page:
Philip Dickel adjusts the uprights
as Joanna Schanz weaves.

SIDE WEAVING

Remember, your weavers must be slimmer or more flexible than your uprights. You want the weavers to weave and not bend or push your uprights inward or outward. You want to be the person who shapes the basket. Do not let the willow weavers shape it. The number of weavers you will need depends on the length of the willows and the number of rows you weave.

"In front of" means the outside of the basket in front of an upright. "Behind" means inside the basket behind an upright.

There are three basic weaves used in the Amana Colony baskets. Four-rod wale and three-rod wale, which are strong weaves, are the first two. The third, French randing, which is a weaker weave, is used to build the height of a basket fast.

FOUR-ROD WALE

You will find four-rod wale at the bottom and top of most large and medium-sized baskets because it is a very strong weave. There are two ways to weave four-rod wale. Amana basketmakers use the two-two or "in front of two, behind two" method.

Select four weavers. Mark one upright with a clothespin, twisty tie or string so that you will know where you began your weaving. When you get back to and past the clothespin or marker you will know that you have completed one row.

Place the first weaver butt end behind the marked upright and weave to the right, in front of two, behind two uprights and out. Place the second weaver tip end behind second upright to the right of the marked upright **but** also under the first weaver and weave the second weaver in front of two, behind two and out. Place the third weaver butt end behind the third upright to the right of the marked upright **but** also under the first two weavers and weave in front of two, behind two and out. Place the fourth weaver tip end behind the fourth upright to the right of the marked upright **but** under the three other weavers and weave in front of two, behind two and out.

Notice that you have four weavers coming from behind four consecutive uprights. You should have this at all times while you are weaving the four-rod wale.

Four-rod wale inserted

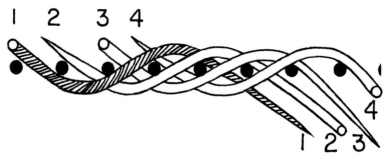

To continue weaving, always pick up the left weaver and weave in front of two, behind two and out. You should be coming out at the next empty space between uprights so that you still have four weavers in a row coming out from behind four consecutive uprights. Pick up the left weaver again and weave in front of two, behind two and out. Continue weaving, replacing willows only when they are in the left-hand position ready to be picked up and woven. Splice butt-end-to-butt-end and tip-end-to-tip-end. Splice with new weaver behind old weaver and not on top of old weaver. When you get back to the marker and past the marker with all four weavers, you have completed one row.

Four-rod wale weaving

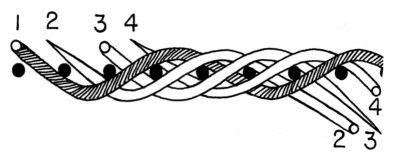

After every two rows, you will want to stop and pound down your rows between the uprights to achieve a tighter woven basket and help compensate for the minor shrinkage that will occur. Also check your tie to be sure it is above the center of your basket. You may need to adjust the tie to help shape your basket.

Weave at least four rows for our sample basket. Pound down, check tie, and shape, before going on to the next step.

Completed four-rod wale

FRENCH RANDING

French randing uses the same number of weavers as uprights. Select 24 weavers the same size in thickness and length. If you find weavers that are not all the same length, line up the tip end and cut the butt end off to match length. Sometimes when you cut the butt end off you are cutting off the fat part of the willow, leaving the thickness of willow you want.

You will be changing directions in inserting and weaving the French randing. Think of the uprights as being numbered from #1 to #24 going clockwise or right to left and think of the weavers being numbered the same.

Insert #1 weaver behind #1 upright and weave to the right in front of two, behind one, and out. Insert #2 weaver behind #2 upright, which is to the left of #1, and weave in front of two, behind one, and out. Insert #3 weaver behind #3 upright, which is to the left of #2, and weave in front of two, behind one, and out. Tie these three weavers together so that it will be easier to insert the last three weavers.

Inserting French randing (beginning)

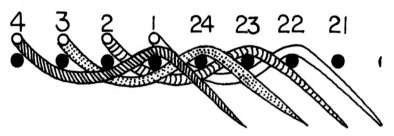

Continue inserting your weavers until you have all but the last three (#22, #23, and #24). Insert the #22 weaver behind #22 upright, **but** be sure you are under #1 weaver, which is coming out from that space, and weave #22 in front of two, behind one, and out. Insert #23 weaver behind #23 upright, **but** be sure you are under #1 and #2 weavers and weave #23 in front of two, behind one, and out. Insert #24 weaver behind #24 upright, **but** be sure that you are under #1, #2, and #3 weavers that are already in place and weave #24 in front of two, behind one, and out. Remove the tie that is on #1, #2, and #3. All 24 weavers are inserted and you are ready to weave row by row.

Inserting the last three French randing weavers

Still think of the weavers being numbered from #1 to #24. To weave a row you can start with any of the weavers and call it #1. You will be weaving clockwise, so #2 weaver will be to the left of #1.

Pick up #1 weaver and weave in front of one, behind one, and out. Pick up #2 weaver and weave in front of one, behind one, and out. Tie these two weavers together. They will be laying on top of #23 and #24. The tie will remind you that you have already used #1 and #2 for this row, and it is #23 and #24 that need to be picked up and woven.

Pick up #3 weaver and weave in front of one, behind one, and out. Pick up #4 weaver and weave in front of one, behind one, and out.

Continue picking up and weaving until you have all 24 weavers woven in front of one, behind one, and out. Pay close attention to weave #23 and #24 correctly. Do not cross #23 and #24 over #1 and #2. Remove tie from #1 and #2. You have completed one row.

Start a second row with a new #1 weaver and continue weaving the French randing row by row until you are to the tip end of your weavers. You can cut the weavers off on the outside of your basket or the inside of your basket.

After every two rows, you will want to stop and pound down your rows between the uprights to achieve a tighter woven basket and help compensate for the minor shrinkage that will occur. Also check your tie to be sure it is above the center of your basket. You may need to adjust the tie to help shape your basket.

French randing mistakes to watch for: Picking up #1 and #2 weavers twice in a row and forgetting #23 and #24. Picking up #1 and #2 weavers twice in a row and also weaving #23 and #24. Weaving #23 and #24 over #1 and #2. Skipping weavers or picking them up out of order.

Completed French randing

This basket by Richard Seifert, Jr. (1895-1980) shows two-color stripe, a French randing variation.

FRENCH RANDING VARIATIONS

Two-color vertical stripe — Insert peeled weaver and weave in front of one, behind one, and out. Insert unpeeled weaver and weave in front of one, behind one, and out. Insert peeled weaver and weave. Insert unpeeled weaver and weave. Continue to insert peeled and unpeeled weavers in an alternating fashion. Remember to insert the last weavers under the first inserted weavers so your pattern will continue the same.

After all French randing weavers have been inserted, weave in front of one, behind one, and out. You will notice a striped look to your French randing.

Two-color spiral — Insert peeled weaver and weave in front of one, behind one, and out. Insert a second peeled weaver and weave in front of one, behind one, and out. Insert unpeeled weaver and weave in front of one, behind one, and out. Insert a second unpeeled weaver and weave in front of one, behind one, and out. Continue inserting two peeled weavers, then two unpeeled weavers in an alternating fashion until all French randing weavers have been inserted. On some baskets, the last six weavers will be inserted three peeled and then three unpeeled.

After all French randing weavers have been inserted, weave in front of one, behind one, and out. You will notice a spiral look to your French randing.

Two-color patch — Insert peeled weaver and weave in front of one, behind one, and out. Insert unpeeled weaver and weave in front of one, behind one, and out. Insert peeled weaver and weave in front of one, behind one, and out. Continue inserting peeled and unpeeled weavers in an alternating fashion until all French randing weavers have been inserted.

When all French randing weavers have been inserted, weave in front of one, behind two, and out. Next row, weave in front of one, behind one, and out. Next row, weave in front of one, behind two, and out. Continue weaving row by row (in front of one, behind one, and out, then in front of one, behind two, and out). You will notice a patchwork look to your French randing.

You can also achieve a two-color patch by weaving one section of two-color vertical stripe French randing, then a second section of two-color vertical stripe French randing, alternating the placement of the peeled and unpeeled willow.

Two-color large spiral — Insert three consecutive peeled weavers and weave each one in front of one, behind one, and out. Insert three consecutive unpeeled weavers and weave each one in front of one, behind one, and out. Continue inserting three peeled and three unpeeled in an alternating fashion.

When all French randing weavers have been inserted, weave in front of one, behind one, and out. You will notice a large spiral forming on the sides of your basket. Increasing the number of weavers in your consecutive count increases the width of your spiral.

62

THREE-ROD WALE

You will find three-rod wale on many of the smaller baskets. It is a strong weave used at the top and bottom.

Select three weavers. Mark one upright with a clothespin, twisty tie, or string so that you will know where you began your weaving. When you get back to and past the clothespin or marker you know that you have completed one row.

Place the first weaver butt end behind the marked upright and weave to the right "in front of two, behind one" uprights, and out. Place the second weaver tip end behind second upright to the right of the marked upright **but** also under the first weaver and weave "in front of two, behind one," and out. Place the third weaver butt end behind the third upright to the right of the marked upright **but** also under the first two weavers and weave in front of two, behind one, and out.

Three-rod wale inserted

Notice that you have three weavers coming from behind three consecutive uprights. You should have this whenever you are weaving the three-rod wale. To continue weaving, always pick up the left weaver and weave in front of two, behind one, and out. You should be coming out at the next empty space between uprights so that you still have three weavers in a row coming out from behind three consecutive uprights. Pick up the left weaver again and weave in front of two, behind one, and out. Continue weaving, replacing willows only when they are in the left-hand position ready to be picked up and woven. Splice butt-end-to-butt-end and tip-end-to-tip-end. Splice side-to-side with new weaver behind old weaver, not new weaver on top of old weaver. When you get back and past the marker with all three weavers you have completed one row.

Three-rod wale weaving

After every two rows, you will want to stop and pound down your rows between the uprights to achieve a tighter woven basket and help compensate for the minor shrinkage that will occur. Also check your tie to be sure it is above the center of your basket. You may need to adjust the tie to help shape your basket.

Weave at least two rows for our sample basket. Pound down, check tie, and shape. You are ready for the turn-down.

Completed Three-rod wale

TURNING THE TOP DOWN

Pound down your basket, untie uprights if still tied up, and do any shaping of your basket that needs to be done. It will be easier to follow the turn-down directions if you number your uprights from #1 to #24 going counter-clockwise (from left to right). Remember, uprights are always uprights even though they are turned down or timbered. Uprights count when you are weaving "in front of" or "behind". So that you will have space to place your last uprights, bend #1, #2, #3, and #4 to the right over a fat round screwdriver and let them stand back up.

#1 upright turns down or timbers to the right, behind two, and out.

#2 upright turns down or timbers to the right, behind two, and out.

#3 upright turns down or timbers to the right, behind two, and out.

#4 upright turns down or timbers to the right, behind two, and out.

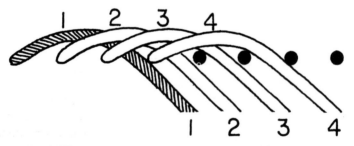

#1 is picked up and weaves in front of two, behind two, and out. (Note: When #1 goes in front of two it should be in front of one turned or timbered upright and one that is standing.) #1 is done weaving. #5 is turned down or timbered behind two and rests beside and behind #1, toward the inside of your basket.

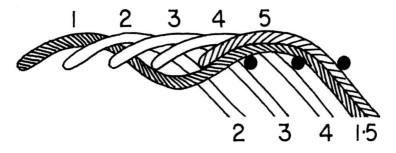

#2 is picked up and weaves in front of two, behind two, and out. Be sure to count the timbered upright when counting the "in front of two". #2 is done weaving. #6 is turned down or timbered behind two and rests beside and behind #2, toward the inside of your basket.

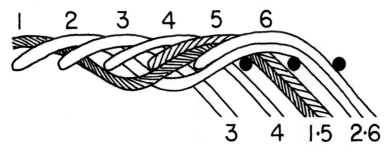

#3 is picked up and weaves in front of two, behind two, and out. #3 is done weaving. #7 timbers down behind two, resting inside of #3.

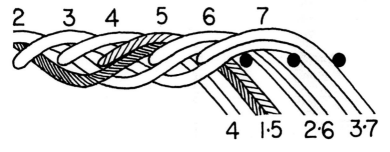

#4 is picked up and weaves in front of two, behind two, and out. #8 timbers down behind two, resting inside of #4. #4 is done weaving. At this point you should have two double uprights turned down and coming out from behind four uprights that are still standing. From this point on you should always have four doubles in a row.

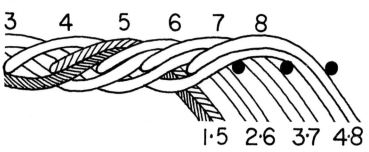

You continue turning down by picking up #5, which is on the inside of #1, and weaving in front of two, behind two, and out. #5 is now done weaving. #9 is timbered down, resting inside of #5. Working your way around the basket, you will be moving the doubles over, leaving a single. It is important to keep the uprights in the correct position when turning them down so that you will be picking up the correct upright to weave with.

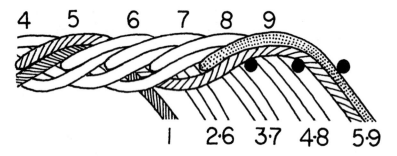

Continue the turn-down by picking up the inside timbered uprights and weaving in front of two, behind two, and out. Timber down the next standing upright, keeping it in the correct position. (Note: Common errors — Picking up the outside timbered upright to weave with, leaving a double behind, and forgetting to timber down an upright.)

You continue turning the uprights down, but when you get close to the end it will be more difficult, and you need to concentrate. #18 is picked up and weaves in front of two, behind two, and comes out between #24, which is still standing, and #1, which is turned down. #22 timbers down and rests inside of #18. You now have two uprights standing.

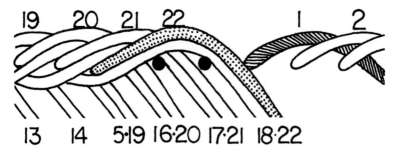

#19 is picked up and weaves in front of two, behind two, and comes out between #1 and #2. You must bring #19 from the inside of your basket and pull it through the opening that was made by bending #1 over the fat screwdriver. #23 timbers down and goes through the same opening, keeping to the inside of #19.

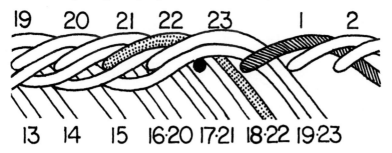

#20 is picked up and weaves in front of two, behind two, and is pulled through the opening between #2 and #3. #24 timbers down behind two, going through the same opening. You now have all the uprights timbered down and only four doubles left.

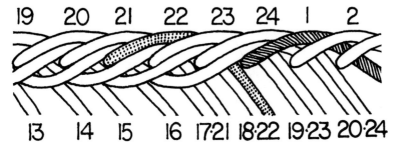

Study your turn-down and see the pattern. Each timbered upright has a picked-up upright resting to the outside. When you pick up and weave #21, #22, #23, and #24, follow the same pattern.

#21 weaves in front of two, behind two, and comes out between #2 and #3, but to the outside of #2. If you put a fat screwdriver on **top** of #2 (where #21 should come out), but under all the other timbered uprights, you can roll #21 to the outside to keep the turn-down pattern.

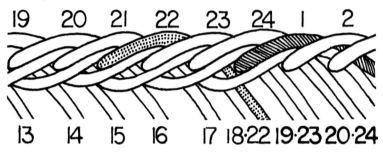

#22 weaves in front of two, behind two, and on top of #3 — and rolls to the outside of #3.

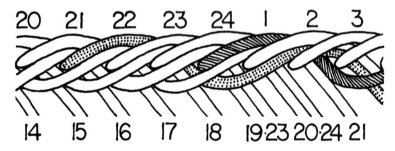

#23 weaves in front of two, behind two, and on top of #4 — and rolls to the outside of #4.

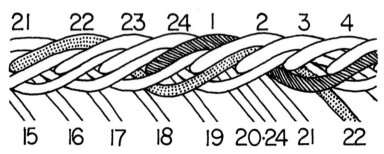

#24 weaves in front of two, behind two, and on top of #5 — and rolls to the outside of #5.

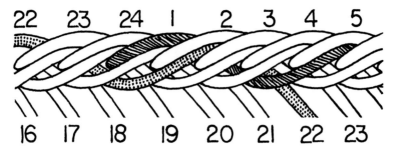

Cut the uprights very short, as they will be resting against another upright and stay in place. Save the cut-off uprights for the removable bottom rim. Turning the top down as instructed will put the minimal amount of stress on your willows.

Completed top turndown

REMOVABLE BOTTOM RIM

All willow baskets made in the Amana Colonies have a removable bottom rim. This is an added weaving and turn-down that keeps the bottom of the basket off the floor or ground. The rim takes the wear and tear of daily use, and when the rim breaks or wears down you can just remove the old rim and replace it with a new rim.

Inserting bottom rim uprights — Turn your basket upside-down so that you can work on the bottom rim. Taper-cut the uprights you just cut off the top of your basket. Insert one upright alongside each basket side upright, making sure the inserted rim upright is into the basket about 1 to 1½ inches. Be sure that the rim upright is alongside the side upright and not poking out the inside or outside of the basket.

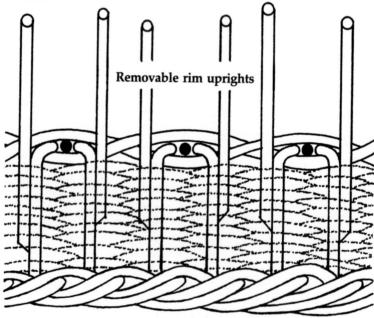

Removable rim uprights

Top of basket

Weaving — When all 24 rim uprights have been inserted, weave two rows of four-rod wale. Make sure you push and pull the weaving nice and tight to the four-rod wale that is already in your basket.

Turning the bottom rim uprights down — Turn down the bottom removable rim with the two-two-two turn-down you have at the top of your basket. Pound down the bottom rim to help tighten it against the side weavers. You are ready for handles.

Basket is upside-down to show completed bottom rim.

HANDLES

TWO SMALL HANDLES ON OPPOSITE SIDES

Handle spokes — Gently bend two fat willows around your knee to make a curved handle without any sharp bends or kinks. Measure the size of the handle spoke by holding the bent willow up to your basket and taper-cutting the ends. Insert both ends of one handle down alongside two uprights of the basket, keeping a couple of uprights between the handle spokes. Push in the handle spoke carefully until there are three to four finger spaces between handle spoke and basket top rim.

Handle wrappers — Select two long, skinny, straight, flawless willows for each handle spoke. Taper-cut butt ends. Insert one handle wrapper butt end into the basket side next to the outside of the handle spokes.

Starting at the tip end of the wrapper, twist and flex the willow so that it becomes flexible and will be able to make sharp turns without breaking. Twist in the same direction. Do not change twisting directions. You will see, hear, and feel the skin of the willow breaking. This is what it should do.

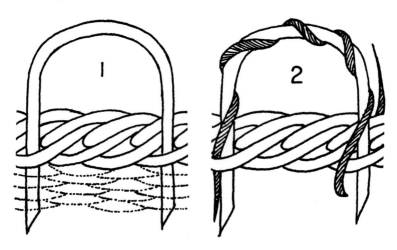

After you have twisted one willow wrapper down to the rim, hold the twist about four to six inches from the rim and start to wrap or snake the twisted willow wrapper around the handle spoke. As you need more willow to wrap around the handle spoke, move up the willow toward the tip end, holding the twist as you move up. Your first snakes or wraps should be about two finger-spaces apart. When you come to the other side of the handle spoke you thread the twisted wrapper through the basket side about two rows from the top, staying to the inside of the handle spokes. Pull through and bring up to wrap back across the handle spoke, following the first wrapper. Thread the end through the basket two rows down and on the inside of the handle spoke. Drop that wrapper. Flex and twist the wrapper on the opposite side of the handle spoke. Wrap or snake the second twisted wrapper, following alongside the first wrapper. After going over and back with both wrappers, your handle should be filled. If not, you may have enough ends left on one of your wrappers to go over one more time.

Steps in a handle wrap — When the handle is filled, weave the ends of your wrappers into the existing weave on the side of the basket.

ONE-LOOP HANDLE

Handle spokes — Select a fat, long willow for your handle spoke. Bend around your knee gently to bend the willow without any sharp bends or kinks. Measure the handle and taper-cut the ends. Insert the handle spoke into your handle, sliding the ends down alongside an upright.

Handle wrappers — Select four to six long, slender, flawless, straight willows to use as handle wrappers. Taper-cut the butt ends and insert one wrapper alongside each side of the handle spoke. Starting at the tip end of the wrapper willow, twist and flex the willow so that it will be flexible enough to wrap around the handle spoke. You will see, hear, and feel the skin of the willow break and twist. This is what it should be doing.

After you have twisted one wrapper willow down to the basket rim, hold the twist about six to eight inches up from the rim and start to wrap or snake around the handle spoke, keeping the spacing about two fingers apart. When you get to the opposite end of the handle spoke, thread the end of the willow through the basket side two rows down from the top. Let the wrapper willow rest inside or outside the basket.

Twist the second willow wrapper that is alongside the second end of the handle spoke. Wrap or snake it around the handle spoke resting next to the first wrapper. Thread the end through the basket side two rows down from the top and let it rest.

Insert two more wrapper willows alongside each side of the handle spoke but also next to the first wrapper willows already in the basket. Twist one wrapper willow over to the other side and thread through, following the existing snakes. Twist the second wrapper willow, snake the handle spoke, thread through and let rest. If your handle is filled completely or as much as you like, you just need to finish wrapping your loose ends. If your handle is not filled as you like, you can add another set of willows on each side, twist, snake, and thread to fill.

Finishing the loose handle wrapper ends — Finish off your wrapper willow ends that you threaded through two rows down by bringing all the wrapper willows up and around the top of the basket and handle in a design or pattern. Weave the wrapper left into the existing basket sides. Do each side the same. Suggested

designs or patterns are sketched. The length of the wrapper determines what you can do. Be creative.

One-loop handle (finishing patterns)

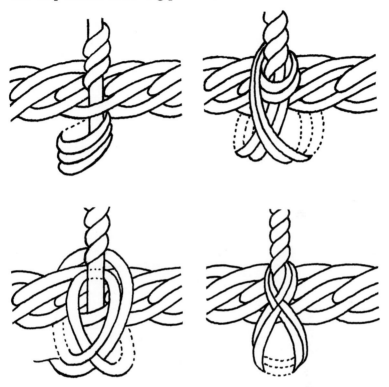

LIDS

If you can make a base, you can make a lid for any of your baskets. Round lids are round bases with a border. Oval lids are oval bases with a border. Usually the border is made by inserting short uprights one per base/lid spoke and turning down with behind one, in front of one, behind one and out. The hard part of making a lid is fitting it on top of your basket or inside your basket. Using your basic knowledge, you can create your own creative lid.

Attach your lid with hinges made from split willows. Handles can be woven into your lid, or fabricated by attaching simple willow rings.

Completed lid

PATTERNS AND ADDITIONAL TECHNIQUES

A collection of traditional Amana Colony willow baskets

After learning about and practicing bases, four-rod wale, French randing, three-rod wale, turning down, removable bottom rims, and handles, you are free to create your own round willow baskets. The following patterns are to introduce you to additional techniques you may find helpful and inspirational. Review the basics whenever needed.

APPLE-PICKER

Reinforces the basic round basket with emphasis on shaping.

Materials:

Base — Six base spokes 9 inches long by ⁵⁄₁₆ inch thick. One weaver split for binding base spokes. Approximately 28 weavers.

Uprights — 24 uprights ⁵⁄₁₆ or ¼ inch thick and at least 38 inches long.

Side-weavers — Approximately 66 weavers for four-rod wale. 48 French randing weavers at least 36 inches long.

Handles — Two short handle spokes and four long, skinny handle wrappers.

Directions:

Base — Weave a simple six-spoke base.

Uprights — Insert two uprights per base spoke, bend over screwdriver, and tie.

Side-weaving — Four-rod wale for 6 rows or 2 inches. After 2 rows of four-rod wale, move your tie up so you can start to flare the sides out.

Insert 24 French randing weavers and weave one set of French randing. After every two rows, pound down and check your tie. You will want the French randing to go straight up and not flare out or come in. You must already be flared out as much as you want to flare when you start the French randing. If you need to guide the sides inward, lower your tie. If you need to flare outward, raise your tie. You can untie your uprights, but watch so that you do not flare outward too much or lose your shaping.

Insert 24 more French randing weavers and weave a second set of French randing. Watch your shaping after pounding down every two rows.

Four-rod wale for 10 rows or 3½ inches. You should have your uprights tied up; keep pulling the tie down so that you are shaping the basket inward. Again, check yourself after every two rows.

Turn down with four-rod turn-down (behind two, in front of two, behind two, and out).

Removable bottom rim — Two rows of four-rod wale and turn down.

Handles — Two handles on one side of the basket side by side.

Use your apple-picker not only for apples, but as a wastebasket or mini-clothes hamper. Use it to gather other vegetables and fruits. The two handles on one side let you hang the basket on your ladder or in your tree, leaving both hands free for picking. The shaped top will keep the apples from falling out while hanging at an angle.

Apple-picker.

STRAWBERRY-PICKER

A smaller version of the apple-picker can be made by starting out with a four-spoke base and scaling down all the other dimensions. The two handles on one side will allow your belt to be threaded through so that the basket hangs at your waist and both hands are free. A four-spoke base uses two spokes inserted into two spokes, sixteen uprights, and sixteen French randing weavers.

Strawberry-picker base (Two spokes inside of two).

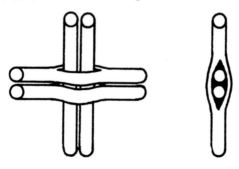

ROUND LAUNDRY BASKET

Large round base, peeled and unpeeled willow with split willow French randing.

Materials:

Base — Eight spokes 14 inches long and $7/16$ inch thick. One weaver split for binding base spokes. Approximately 48 unpeeled weavers and 16 peeled weavers.

Uprights — 32 uprights, unpeeled, $5/16$ inch thick, and at least 34 inches long.

Side-weavers — Approximately 40 unpeeled weavers for four-rod wale. 16 fat, unpeeled weavers split in half for the 32 French randing weavers.

Handles — Two short handle spokes and four skinny handle wrappers.

Large round laundry base spokes (four inside four)

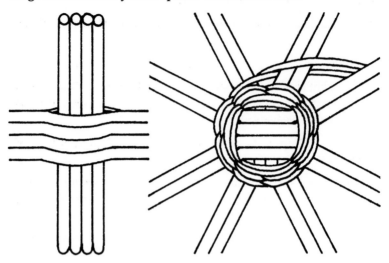

Twining between base spokes

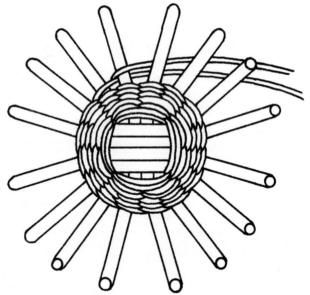

Directions:

Base — Four base spokes inserted into four spokes. Bind together with split weavers by twining over four for three rows. With same split weavers continue twining, but go between two base spokes, starting to spread the base spokes apart. Twine two rows. Replace the split willows with tip ends of two weavers and twine between each base spoke. Remember to splice a new tip end in when a weaver gets too fat. When you have enough room and the base spokes are evenly spaced, start double-twining.

You will want to introduce the tip end of a peeled willow and keep using peeled willows for two or three rows. When you are ready to go back to unpeeled willows, just insert an unpeeled willow when the time comes to replace or splice in a new weaver. Complete your base and trim.

Uprights — Insert two uprights per base spoke. Bend up over a screwdriver and tie.

Side-weaving — Four-rod wale for three rows or 1½ inches.

Split the 16 French randing weavers and insert all 32 split weavers into basket. French rand till weavers are at tip end.

Four-rod wale for two rows or 1½ inches.

Turn down using four-rod turn-down.

Removable bottom rim.

Handles — Two short handles on opposite sides.

If you do not hang clothes outside, you might use this large basket for magazines, toys, or an assortment of plants. Remember — baskets are made to be used!

SMALL OVAL EASTER BASKET

Oval base, peeled willow, and three-rod turn down.

Materials: All peeled willow.

Base — Three ¼ inch thick by 8 inches for your length. Five ¼ inch thick by 5 inches for your width. Two ¼ inch thick by 3 inches for your spacers. One split weaver to bind together base spokes. Approximately 24 weavers.

Uprights — 24 uprights ¼ inch thick and at least 30 inches long.

Side-weavers — Approximately 18 for three-rod wale. 24 French randing at least 24 inches long.

Handle — One loop handle.

Directions:

Base — Insert the three length spokes into the five width spokes. Insert the two spacers, one on each side of the three length spokes. Arrange as shown in diagram below.

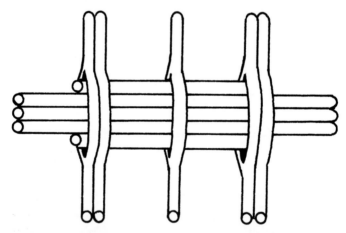

Base spoke arrangement — Split one long willow in half. Using one half of the split willow, bind together the base spokes, starting on one end and ending at the middle width spoke. Make sure you have an "X" on the top and bottom where the width and length spokes cross. The middle width spoke should have only half of an "X". Wrap to center spoke and tuck wrapper end under so it will not unwrap. Using the other half of the split willow, bind together the base spokes starting at the opposite end and ending at the middle width base spoke, completing the "X". Pre-bend the base spokes as shown in diagram below.

Binding the base spokes together

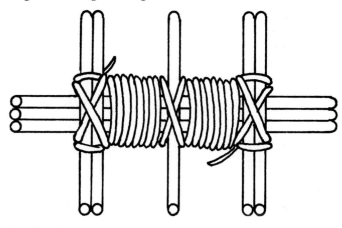

Pre-bending base spokes

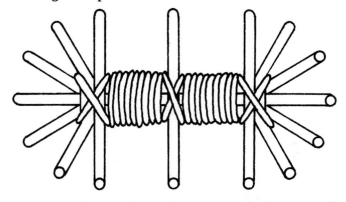

Twining an oval base — Start with two tip ends which we will call "A pair" and twine between each spoke until you get to the opposite end, where you drop "A pair". Start two new tip ends, which we will call "B pair" and twine between the spokes until you get back to "A pair". Drop "B pair" and pick up "A pair" and weave. When weavers become too fat, splice with tip of new weaver. Continue chasing with the "A pair" and "B pair" until your base spokes are evenly spaced and there is enough room for double twining.

Twining with A pair and B pair weavers.

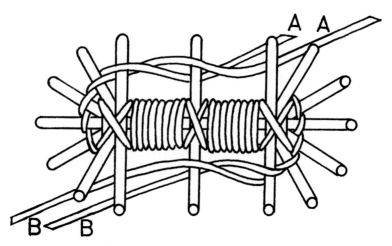

Double twining oval base — When one of the pairs of weavers (either A or B) comes around to meet the other pair, use the skinnier weavers as the skinny weaver in double twining. Use the fatter weaver as the fat weaver in double twining. Remember to add new tip end weavers when necessary so that you always have a skinny weaver with a fat weaver. Keep the skinny weaver towards the center of the base. Weave until the base spokes are filled. Trim your base.

Uprights — Insert as shown in diagram below. Bend and tie up.

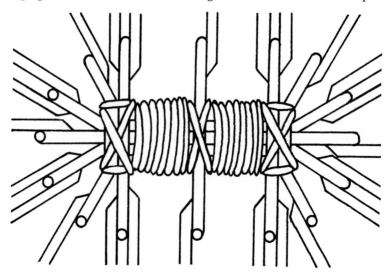

Side-weavers — Three rows of three-rod wale or ¾ inch.

One section of French randing as follows: Insert weaver and weave in front of one, behind one, and out. Insert weaver and weave in front of one, behind one, and out. Do not forget to insert weavers in a clockwise direction, or from right to left. Continue inserting the French randing weavers. Remember to insert the last three weavers under the first three inserted weavers so that your pattern will continue the same. After all French randing weavers have been inserted, weave in front of one, behind one, and out.

Two rows of three-rod wale or ½ inch.

Turn down using a three-rod turn-down (behind one, in front of two, behind one, and out). Number your uprights from one to twenty-four going counterclockwise, or from left to right. #1 upright bends over screwdriver and goes behind one. #2 upright bends over screwdriver and goes behind one. #3 upright bends over screwdriver and goes behind one.

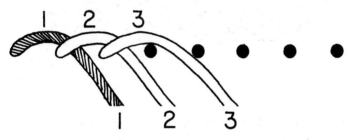

Pick up #1 and weave in front of two, behind one, and out. #1 is done with turn-down. #4 is timbered down behind one, resting to the inside of #1.

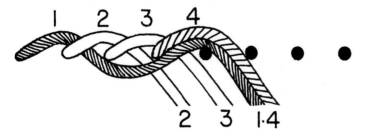

Pick up #2 and weave in front of two, behind one, and out. #2 is done with turn-down. #5 is timbered down behind one, resting to the inside of #2.

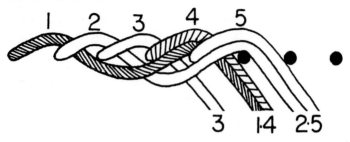

Pick up #3 and weave in front of two, behind one, and out. #3 is done with turn-down. #6 is timbered down behind one, resting to the inside of #3.

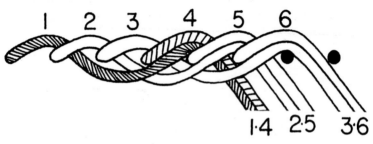

Continue turning down by picking up the next upright (which would be #4) and weave in front of two, behind one, and out. Timber down the next standing upright (which would be #7), keeping it to the inside of #4. Work your way around the top rim until all uprights have completed the sequence behind one, in front of two, behind one, and out. Trim and save the uprights to be used on the removable bottom rim.

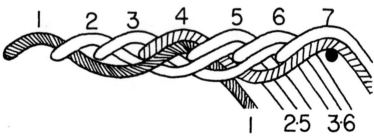

Three-rod wale ending

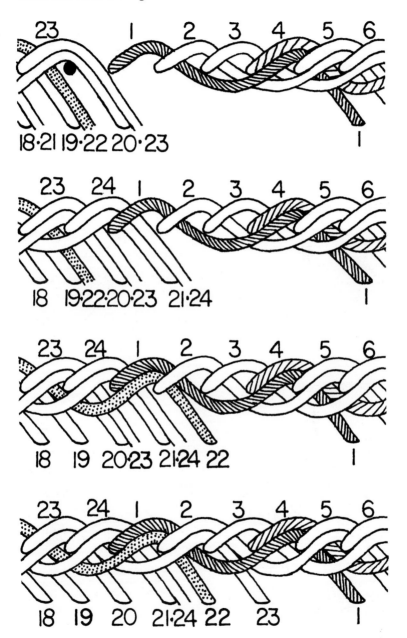

Completed three-rod wale top turn-down

Removable bottom rim using the three-rod wale and three-rod turn-down.

Handle — Single handle using peeled wrappers.

You will find many uses for this little oval Easter basket, even if the Easter bunny does not stop at your house.

OVAL COMMUNITY KITCHEN BASKET

Market basket using a wooden handle.

Materials: Peeled or unpeeled or a combination - your choice.

Base — Three 14 inches by ⁵⁄₁₆ inch thick length spokes.
Five 10 inches by ⁶⁄₁₆ inch thick width spokes.
Two 5½ inches by ⁵⁄₁₆ inch spacers.
One split willow for binding.
Approximately 30 weavers.

Uprights — 28 willows that are about ¼ to ⅜ inch thick and at least 38 inches long.

Side-weavers — Approximately 28 weavers for four-rod wale. 26 weavers for French randing at least 27 inches long.

Handle — One wooden handle 1 inch wide by ³⁄₁₆ inch and 28 inches long.

Directions:

Base — Weave oval base with base spokes arranged as shown in diagram. Refer to oval-base weaving detailed in instructions for small oval Easter basket.

Oval community kitchen basket (Base spokes arrangement and uprights placement).

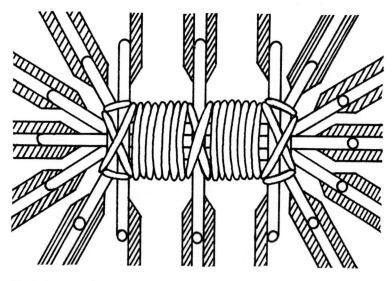

Uprights — Insert 28 uprights as diagrammed. Bend and tie up.

Side-weavers — Weave three rows of four-rod wale or ⅞ inch.

French randing — Uses only 26 weavers. From this point on, treat the two uprights that come from the middle base spoke as one upright, with the wooden handle between the uprights. You will find it helpful to insert the handle and tie or tape the two uprights to the handle. Insert the 26 weavers and weave French randing for about 2 inches.

Six rows or two inches of four-rod wale. Do not forget to treat the two uprights coming out of the middle base spoke as one, with the handle between the uprights.

Turn down — Cut off the upright to the right of the handle and save for removable bottom rim. Turn down the top with the remaining 26 uprights with four-rod wale turn-down (behind two, in front of two, behind two, and out). Trim and save uprights for removable bottom rim.

Removable bottom rim — Insert 28 bottom rim uprights and weave a couple rows of four-rod wale, keeping the rows close to the bottom four-rod wale already in your basket. Turn down rim and trim.

Peg handle in place below two rows of the four-rod wale.

Carry your oval basket proudly to market, to the garden, and on picnics, or keep it in the house usefully holding sewing, knitting, plants, etc. Make another oval, creatively combining peeled and unpeeled willows.

GLOSSARY

OF TERMS USED IN AMANA COLONY WILLOW BASKETRY

Back: The outside curve of a willow rod.

Base: Bottom of a basket.

Belly: The inside curve of a willow rod.

Butt: The fat end of a willow rod.

Chasing: Technique in weaving. One weaver or set of weavers follows another weaver or set of weavers.

Double twining: Technique in weaving. One weaver is skinny and one weaver is fat. The two weavers are held together as one when twining.

Four-rod wale: Technique in weaving. Four weavers are used, woven one at a time, in front of two, behind two, and out.

French randing: Technique in weaving. Same number of weavers as uprights. Each weaver is woven one at a time. There are several variations of French randing.

Mulching: Covering the ground with straw, grass clippings, shredded paper, or commercial mulch to control weeds, enrich the soil, and keep the ground moist.

Slewing: A weaving technique seldom used in the Amana Colonies.

Spokes: Base supports. They extend outward from center of base.

Taper-cut: Cutting willow rod at a slant.

Three-rod wale: Technique in weaving. Three weavers are used, woven one at a time, in front of two, behind one, and out.

Timber down: Bending an upright down as a tree would fall when cut.

Tip: The skinny end or top of a willow rod.

Turn down: Ending the use of the uprights by timbering down. The top of a basket or the bottom rim of a basket.

Twining: Technique in weaving. Two weavers are used, weaving one at a time, under and over. A twist is formed between spokes or uprights.

Uprights: Side stakes of a basket around which weavers are woven.

Weavers: Material used to wind or intertwine around uprights.

Community kitchen garden baskets. Circa 1900s.

BIBLIOGRAPHY

Cary, Mara. *Basic Baskets*. Boston: Houghton Mifflin Co., 1975.

Hart, Carol and Dan. *Natural Basketry*. New York: Watson-Guptill, 1975.

Knock, A.G. *Willow Basketry*. Takoma Park: Dryad, 1979.

Teleki, Gloria Roth. *Baskets of Rural America*. New York: E P Dutton, 1975.

Teleki, Gloria Roth. *Collecting Traditional American Basketry*. New York: E P Dutton, 1979.

Tod, Osma Gallinger. *Earth Basketry*. No city listed: Orange Judd Publishing, 1933.

Will, Christoph. *International Basketry for Weavers and Collectors*. Exton: Schiffer Publishing Ltd., 1985.

Wright, Dorothy. *The Complete Book of Baskets and Basketry*. North Pomfret: David and Charles, 1983.

PUBLICATIONS

"The Basketmaker Quarterly": MKS Publications Inc. P.O. Box 005, Belleville, MI 48111.

"The News Basket": La Plantz Press. 899 Bayside Cutoff, Bayside, CA 95524. (Note: Oct. 1984 Vol. 1 No. 3 has a good article on English willow.)

Inside back cover: Surrounded by baskets she has made, Kathy Kellenberger is picking out willows to be used in a basket. Buildings in the background are her chicken house, at right, and a shed, both typical of architectural styles for Amana out-buildings.

Back Cover: Joanna Schanz holds the willow basket that was selected for the Basketry Link Exhibition. In the background is her 1862 sandstone home in West Amana. Lidded laundry hamper is of Iowa peeled willows and unpeeled Wisconsin willows, a wedding gift for her daughter and husband from Wisconsin. Other baskets are an assortment of styles and shapes by Joanna.